Holt McDougal Mathematics

Grade 8
Homework and Practice
Workbook

HOLT McDOUGAL

HOUGHTON MIFFLIN HARCOURT

COMMON
CORE
EDITION

Printed in the U.S.A.

ISBN   978-0-547-68667-7

4 5 6 7 8 9 10   1689   20 19 18 17 16 15 14 13 12

4500362419   ^ B C D E F G

Contents

LESSON 1

Rational Numbers

Practice B: Rational Numbers

Simplify.

1. $\dfrac{6}{9}$
_____

2. $\dfrac{48}{96}$
_____

3. $\dfrac{13}{52}$
_____

4. $-\dfrac{7}{28}$
_____

5. $\dfrac{15}{40}$
_____

6. $-\dfrac{4}{48}$
_____

7. $-\dfrac{14}{63}$
_____

8. $\dfrac{12}{72}$
_____

Write each decimal as a fraction in simplest form.

9. 0.72
_____

10. 0.058
_____

11. −1.65
_____

12. 2.1
_____

13. 0.036
_____

14. −4.06
_____

15. 2.305
_____

16. 0.0064
_____

17. −0.60
_____

18. 6.95
_____

19. 0.016
_____

20. 0.0005
_____

Write each fraction as a decimal.

21. $\dfrac{1}{8}$
_____

22. $\dfrac{8}{3}$
_____

23. $\dfrac{14}{15}$
_____

24. $\dfrac{16}{5}$
_____

25. $\dfrac{11}{16}$
_____

26. $\dfrac{7}{9}$
_____

27. $\dfrac{4}{5}$
_____

28. $\dfrac{31}{25}$
_____

29. Make up a fraction that cannot be simplified that has 24 as its denominator.

_____

Holt McDougal Mathematics

Rational Numbers

LESSON 2

Practice B: Multiplying Rational Numbers

Multiply. Write each answer in simplest form.

1. $8\left(\dfrac{3}{4}\right)$

2. $-6\left(\dfrac{9}{18}\right)$

3. $-9\left(\dfrac{5}{6}\right)$

4. $-6\left(-\dfrac{7}{12}\right)$

5. $-\dfrac{5}{18}\left(\dfrac{8}{15}\right)$

6. $\dfrac{7}{12}\left(\dfrac{14}{21}\right)$

7. $-\dfrac{1}{9}\left(\dfrac{27}{24}\right)$

8. $-\dfrac{1}{11}\left(-\dfrac{3}{2}\right)$

9. $\dfrac{7}{20}\left(-\dfrac{15}{28}\right)$

10. $\dfrac{16}{25}\left(-\dfrac{18}{32}\right)$

11. $\dfrac{1}{9}\left(\dfrac{18}{17}\right)$

12. $\dfrac{17}{20}\left(-\dfrac{12}{34}\right)$

13. $-4\left(2\dfrac{1}{6}\right)$

14. $\dfrac{3}{4}\left(1\dfrac{3}{8}\right)$

15. $3\dfrac{1}{5}\left(\dfrac{2}{3}\right)$

16. $-\dfrac{5}{6}\left(2\dfrac{1}{2}\right)$

Multiply.

17. $-2(-5.2)$

18. $0.53(0.04)$

19. $(-7)(-3.9)$

20. $-2(8.13)$

21. $0.02(-4.62)$

22. $0.5(-7.8)$

23. $(-0.41)(-8.5)$

24. $(-8)(6.3)$

25. $15(-0.05)$

26. $(-3.04)(-1.7)$

27. $10(-0.09)$

28. $(-0.8)(-0.15)$

29. Travis painted for $6\dfrac{2}{3}$ hours. He received \$27 an hour for his work. How much was Travis paid for doing this painting job?

_____

Holt McDougal Mathematics

Rational Numbers

LESSON 3

Practice B: Dividing Rational Numbers

Divide. Write each answer in simplest form.

1. $\dfrac{1}{5} \div \dfrac{3}{10}$

2. $-\dfrac{5}{8} \div \dfrac{3}{4}$

3. $\dfrac{1}{4} \div \dfrac{1}{8}$

4. $-\dfrac{2}{3} \div \dfrac{4}{15}$

5. $1\dfrac{2}{9} \div 1\dfrac{2}{3}$

6. $-\dfrac{7}{10} \div \left(\dfrac{2}{5}\right)$

7. $\dfrac{6}{11} \div \dfrac{3}{22}$

8. $\dfrac{4}{9} \div \left(-\dfrac{8}{15}\right)$

9. $\dfrac{3}{8} \div -15$

10. $-\dfrac{5}{6} \div 12$

11. $6\dfrac{1}{2} \div 1\dfrac{5}{8}$

12. $-\dfrac{9}{10} \div 6$

Find each quotient.

13. $24.35 \div 0.5$

14. $2.16 \div 0.04$

15. $3.16 \div 0.02$

16. $7.32 \div 0.3$

17. $87.36 \div 0.6$

18. $79.36 \div 0.8$

19. $4.27 \div 0.007$

20. $63.81 \div 0.9$

21. $1.23 \div 0.003$

22. $62.46 \div 0.09$

23. $21.12 \div 0.4$

24. $82.68 \div 0.06$

Evaluate each expression for the given value of the variable.

25. $\dfrac{18}{x}$ for $x = 0.12$

26. $\dfrac{10.8}{x}$ for $x = 0.03$

27. $\dfrac{9.18}{x}$ for $x = -1.2$

28. A can of fruit contains $3\dfrac{1}{2}$ cups of fruit. The suggested serving size is $\dfrac{1}{2}$ cup. How many servings are in the can of fruit?

Holt McDougal Mathematics

Rational Numbers

LESSON 4

Practice B: Adding and Subtracting with Unlike Denominators

Add or subtract.

1. $\dfrac{2}{3} + \dfrac{1}{2}$

2. $\dfrac{3}{5} + \dfrac{1}{3}$

3. $\dfrac{3}{4} - \dfrac{1}{3}$

4. $\dfrac{1}{2} - \dfrac{5}{9}$

_____ _____ _____ _____

5. $\dfrac{5}{16} - \dfrac{5}{8}$

6. $\dfrac{7}{9} + \dfrac{5}{6}$

7. $\dfrac{7}{8} - \dfrac{1}{4}$

8. $\dfrac{5}{6} - \dfrac{3}{8}$

_____ _____ _____ _____

9. $2\dfrac{7}{8} + 3\dfrac{5}{12}$

10. $1\dfrac{2}{9} + 2\dfrac{1}{18}$

11. $3\dfrac{2}{3} - 1\dfrac{3}{5}$

12. $1\dfrac{5}{6} + \left(-2\dfrac{3}{4}\right)$

_____ _____ _____ _____

13. $8\dfrac{1}{3} - 3\dfrac{5}{9}$

14. $5\dfrac{1}{3} + 1\dfrac{11}{12}$

15. $7\dfrac{1}{4} + \left(-2\dfrac{5}{12}\right)$

16. $5\dfrac{2}{5} - 7\dfrac{3}{10}$

_____ _____ _____ _____

Evaluate each expression for the given value of the variable.

17. $2\dfrac{3}{8} + x$ for $x = 1\dfrac{5}{6}$

18. $x - \dfrac{2}{5}$ for $x = \dfrac{1}{3}$

19. $x - \dfrac{3}{10}$ for $x = \dfrac{3}{7}$

_____ _____ _____

20. $1\dfrac{5}{8} + x$ for $x = -2\dfrac{1}{6}$

21. $x - \dfrac{3}{4}$ for $x = \dfrac{1}{6}$

22. $x - \dfrac{3}{10}$ for $x = \dfrac{1}{2}$

_____ _____ _____

23. Ana worked $6\dfrac{1}{2}$ h on Monday, $5\dfrac{3}{4}$ h on Tuesday and $7\dfrac{1}{6}$ h on Friday. How many total hours did she work these three days?

_____

Holt McDougal Mathematics

LESSON 5

Rational Numbers

Practice B: Solving Equations with Rational Numbers

Solve.

1. $x + 6.8 = 12.19$

2. $y - 10.24 = 5.3$

3. $0.05w = 6.25$

_____

_____

_____

4. $\dfrac{a}{9.05} = 8.2$

5. $-12.41 + x = -0.06$

6. $\dfrac{d}{-8.4} = -10.2$

_____

_____

_____

7. $-2.89 = 1.7m$

8. $n - 8.09 = -11.65$

9. $\dfrac{x}{5.4} = -7.18$

_____

_____

_____

10. $\dfrac{7}{9} + x = 1\dfrac{1}{9}$

11. $\dfrac{6}{11}y = -\dfrac{18}{22}$

12. $\dfrac{7}{10}d = \dfrac{21}{20}$

_____

_____

_____

13. $x - \left(-\dfrac{9}{14}\right) = \dfrac{5}{7}$

14. $x - \dfrac{15}{21} = 2\dfrac{6}{7}$

15. $-\dfrac{8}{15}a = \dfrac{9}{10}$

_____

_____

_____

16. A recipe calls for $2\dfrac{1}{3}$ cups of flour and $1\dfrac{1}{4}$ cups of sugar. If the

recipe is tripled, how much flour and sugar will be needed?

_____

17. Daniel filled the gas tank in his car with 14.6 gal of gas. He then
drove 284.7 mi before needing to fill up his tank with gas again.
How many miles did the car get to a gallon of gasoline?

_____

Holt McDougal Mathematics

Name _____ Date _____ Class _____

Rational Numbers
Practice B: Solving Two-Step Equations

1. The school purchased baseball equipment and uniforms for a total cost of $1762. The equipment costs $598 and the uniforms were $24.25 each. How many uniforms did the school purchase?

_____

_____

_____

_____

_____

2. Carla runs 4 miles every day. She jogs from home to the school track, which is $\frac{3}{4}$ mile away. She then runs laps around the $\frac{1}{4}$-mile track. Carla then jogs home. How many laps does she run at the school?

_____

_____

_____

_____

_____

Solve.

3. $\dfrac{a+5}{3}=12$

4. $\dfrac{x+2}{4}=-2$

5. $\dfrac{y-4}{6}=-3$

6. $\dfrac{k+1}{8}=7$

_____

_____

_____

_____

7. $0.5x-6=-4$

8. $\dfrac{x}{2}+3=-4$

9. $\dfrac{1}{5}n+3=6$

10. $2a-7=-9$

_____

_____

_____

_____

11. $\dfrac{3x-1}{4}=2$

12. $-7.8=4.4+2r$

13. $\dfrac{-4w+5}{-3}=-7$

14. $1.3-5r=7.4$

_____

_____

_____

_____

15. A phone call costs $0.58 for the first 3 minutes and $0.15 for each additional minute. If the total charge for the call was $4.78, how many minutes was the call?

_____

16. Seventeen less than four times a number is twenty-seven. Find the number.

_____

Holt McDougal Mathematics

LESSON 1

Graphs and Functions

Practice B: Ordered Pairs

Determine whether each ordered pair is a solution of $y = 4 + 2x$.

1. (1, 1)   2. (2, 8)   3. (0, 4)   4. (8, 2)

_____   _____   _____   _____

Determine whether each ordered pair is a solution of $y = 3x - 2$.

5. (1, 1)   6. (3, 7)   7. (5, 15)   8. (6, 16)

_____   _____   _____   _____

Use the given values to complete the table of solutions.

9. $y = x + 5$ for $x = 0, 1, 2, 3, 4$

x	x + 5	y	(x, y)
0			
1			
2			
3			
4			

10. $y = 3x + 1$ for $x = 1, 2, 3, 4, 5$

x	3x + 1	y	(x, y)
1			
2			
3			
4			
5			

11. $y = 2x + 6$ for $x = 0, 1, 2, 3, 4$

x	2x + 6	y	(x, y)
0			
1			
2			
3			
4			

12. $y = 4x - 2$ for $x = 2, 4, 6, 8, 10$

x	4x - 2	y	(x, y)
2			
4			
6			
8			
10			

13. Alexis opened a savings account with a $120 deposit. Each week she will put $20 into the account. The equation that gives the total amount t in her account is $t = 120 + 20w$, where w is the number of weeks since she opened the account. How much money will Alexis have in her savings account after 5 weeks?

_____

Name _____ Date _____ Class_____

Graphs and Functions

Practice B: Graphing on a Coordinate Plane

Give the coordinates and quadrant of each point.

1. *F*
2. *X*

_____   _____

3. *T*
4. *B*

_____   _____

5. *D*
6. *R*

_____   _____

7. *H*
8. *Y*

_____   _____

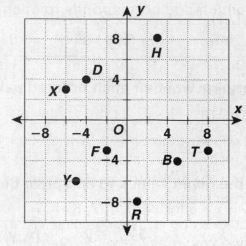

Graph each point on a coordinate plane.

9. $A(2\frac{1}{2}, 1)$ 10. $B(0, 4)$

11. $C(2, -1.5)$ 12. $D(-2, 3.5)$

13. $E(-2\frac{1}{3}, 0)$ 14. $F(-1\frac{1}{2}, -3)$

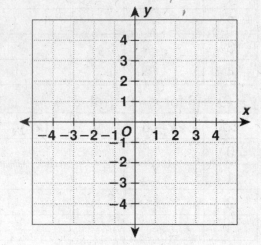

Find the distance between each pair of points.

15. *A* and *B*   16. *C* and *D*

_____   _____

17. *D* and *E*   18. *E* and *F*

_____   _____

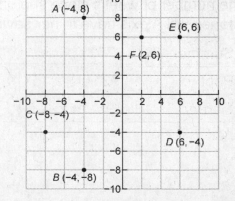

Name _____ Date _____ Class_____

LESSON 3 Graphs and Functions

Practice B: Interpreting Graphs

The table gives the speed of three dogs in mi/h at the given times. Tell which dog corresponds to each situation described below.

Time	5:00	5:01	5:02	5:03	5:04
Dog 1	0	1	12	0	0
Dog 2	5	23	4	0	0
Dog 3	14	0	18	2	9

1. Leshaan walks his dog. Then he lets the dog off the leash and it runs around the yard. Then they go into the house and the dog stands eating from his dog dish and drinking from his water bowl. _____

2. Luke's dog is chasing its tail. Then it stops and pants. The dog then runs to the backyard fence and walks along the fence, barking at a neighbor. Then it runs to Luke at the back door. _____

Tell which graph corresponds to each situation in Exercises 1–2.

3.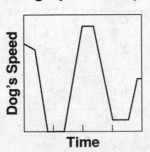

4.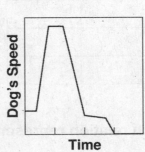

_____   _____

5. Create a graph that illustrates the temperature inside the car.

Location	Temperature on Arrival	Temperature on Departure
Home	—	74° at 8:30
Summer job	77° at 9:00	128° at 12:05
Pool	92° at 12:15	136° at 2:30
Library	95° at 2:40	77° at 5:10

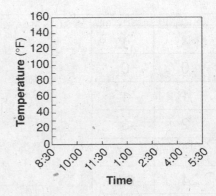

© Houghton Mifflin Harcourt Publishing Company

9   Holt McDougal Mathematics

Name _____ Date _____ Class_____

LESSON 4

Graphs and Functions

Practice B: Functions

Complete the table and graph each function.

1. $y = -2x + 5$

x	$-2x + 5$	y
-2		
-1		
0		
1		
2		

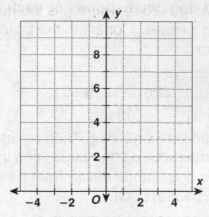

2. $y = x - 2$

x	$x - 2$	y
-2		
-1		
0		
1		
2		

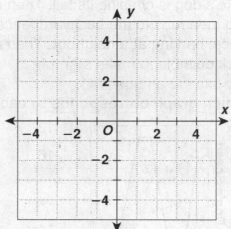

Determine if each relation represents a function.

3. $y = \frac{1}{3}x - \frac{2}{5}$

4.

x	1	2	1	2
y	6	5	-6	-5

_____

5.

x	y
0	0
1	-1
2	-8
3	-27
4	-64

6.

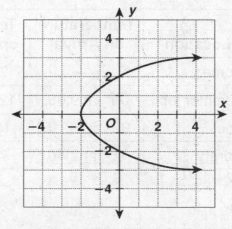

_____   _____

LESSON 5 Graphs and Functions
Practice B: Equations, Tables, and Graphs

1. The amount of water in a tank being filled is represented by the equation $g = 20m$, where g is the number of gallons in the tank after m minutes. Complete the table and sketch a graph of the equation.

m	20m	g
0		
1		
2		
3		
4		

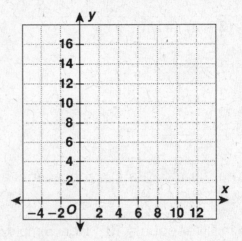

2. Use the table to make a graph and to write an equation.

x	0	2	5	8	12
y	4	6	9	12	16

_____

3. Use the graph to make a table and to write an equation.

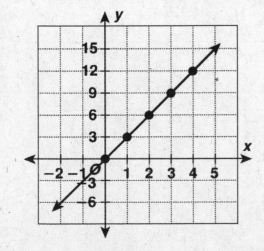

x					
y					

_____

Holt McDougal Mathematics

LESSON 1
Exponents and Roots
Practice B: Integer Exponents

Simplify. Write in decimal form.

1. 10^{-3} 　　　　 2. 10^3 　　　　 3. 10^{-5} 　　　　 4. 10^{-2}

_____　　_____　　_____　　_____

5. 10^0 　　　　 6. 10^4 　　　　 7. 10^1 　　　　 8. 10^5

_____　　_____　　_____　　_____

Simplify.

9. $(-6)^{-2}$ 　　　　 10. $(-9)^{-3}$ 　　　　 11. 2^{-5}

_____　　_____　　_____

12. $(-3)^{-4}$ 　　　　 13. $(-12)^{-1}$ 　　　　 14. 6^{-3}

_____　　_____　　_____

15. $10 - (3 + 2)^0 + 2^{-1}$ 　　　　 16. $15 + (-6)^0 - 3^{-2}$

_____　　　　　　_____

17. $6(8 - 2)^0 + 4^{-2}$ 　　　　 18. $2^{-2} + (-4)^{-1}$

_____　　　　　　_____

19. $3(1 - 4)^{-2} + 9^{-1} + 12^0$ 　　　　 20. $9^0 + 64(3 + 5)^{-2}$

_____　　　　　　_____

21. One milliliter equals 10^{-3} liter. Simplify 10^{-3}.

_____

22. The volume of a cube is 10^6 cubic feet. Simplify 10^6.

_____

　　　　 Holt McDougal Mathematics

LESSON 2

Exponents and Roots

Practice B: Properties of Exponents

Multiply. Write the product as one power.

1. $10^5 \cdot 10^7$

2. $x^9 \cdot x^8$

3. $14^7 \cdot 14^9$

4. $12^6 \cdot 12^8$

_____

5. $y^{12} \cdot y^{10}$

6. $15^9 \cdot 15^{14}$

7. $(-11)^{20} \cdot (-11)^{10}$

8. $(-a)^6 \cdot (-a)^7$

_____

Divide. Write the quotient as one power.

9. $\dfrac{12^9}{12^2}$

10. $\dfrac{(-11)^{12}}{(-11)^8}$

11. $\dfrac{x^5}{x^{10}}$

12. $\dfrac{16^{10}}{16^2}$

_____

13. $\dfrac{17^{19}}{17^2}$

14. $\dfrac{14^{13}}{14^{15}}$

15. $\dfrac{23^{17}}{23^9}$

16. $\dfrac{(-a)^{12}}{(-a)^7}$

_____

Simplify.

17. $(6^2)^4$

18. $(2^4)^{-3}$

19. $(3^5)^{-1}$

20. $(y^5)^2$

_____

21. $(9^{-2})^3$

22. $(10^0)^3$

23. $(x^4)^{-2}$

24. $(5^{-2})^0$

_____

Write the product or quotient as one power.

25. $\dfrac{w^{12}}{w^3}$

26. $d^8 \cdot d^5$

27. $(-15)^5 \cdot (-15)^{10}$

_____

28. Jefferson High School has a student body of 6^4 students. Each class has approximately 6^2 students. How many classes does the school have? Write the answer as one power.

_____

29. Write the expression for a number used as a factor fifteen times being multiplied by a number used as a factor ten times. Then, write the product as one power.

_____

LESSON 3	**Exponents and Roots**

Practice B: Scientific Notation

Write each number in standard notation.

1. 2.54×10^2

2. 6.7×10^{-2}

3. 1.14×10^3

4. 3.8×10^{-1}

5. 7.53×10^{-3}

6. 5.6×10^4

7. 9.1×10^5

8. 6.08×10^{-4}

9. 8.59×10^5

10. 3.331×10^6

11. 7.21×10^{-3}

12. 5.88×10^{-4}

Write each number in scientific notation.

13. 75,000,000

14. 208

15. 907,100

16. 56

17. 0.093

18. 0.00006

19. 0.00852

20. 0.0505

21. 0.003007

22. 5226

23. 0.04

24. 98,856

25. Jupiter is about 778,120,000 kilometers from the Sun. Write this number in scientific notation.

26. The *E. coli* bacterium is about 5×10^{-7} meters wide. A hair is about 1.7×10^{-5} meters wide. Which is wider, the bacterium or the hair?

LESSON 4 — Exponents and Roots

Practice B: Operating with Scientific Notation

Write your answer in scientific notation.

1. Rhode Island is the smallest state. It has an area of approximately 1.55×10^3 square miles. Alaska is the largest state. The area of Alaska is 4.28×10^2 times greater than the area of Rhode Island.

   What is the approximate area of Alaska in square miles?

   _____

2. In 2008, the total trade between the United States and Japan was $\$2.04 \times 10^{11}$. The total trade between the U.S. and Australia was $\$3.28 \times 10^{10}$.

   How many times greater was the trade with Japan than the trade with Australia? _____

3. Between 2008 and 2009, Americans spent $\$8.48 \times 10^8$ on baby food. During the same period, Americans spent $\$4.52 \times 10^9$ on ice cream.

   How much did Americans spend altogether on ice cream and baby food between 2008 and 2009? _____

4. Wrangell-St. Elias National Park in Alaska is the largest national park. It includes approximately 1.32×10^7 acres. Thaddeus Kosciuszcko National Memorial in Pennsylvania is the smallest national park. It is located on approximately 2.0×10^{-2} acres.

   How many times greater is the area of Wrangell-St. Alias National Park than Thaddeus Kosciuszcko National Memorial?

   _____

5. Approximately 3.25×10^6 cubic yards of material were used to build Boulder Dam on the Arizona-Nevada border. The New Cornelia Tailings Dam in Arizona used 2.74×10^8 cubic yards of material.

   How many more cubic yards of material were used to build the Cornelia Tailings Dam than Boulder Dam? _____

LESSON
5

Exponents and Roots

Practice B: Squares and Square Roots

Find the two square roots of each number.

1. 36

2. 81

3. 49

4. 100

_____

5. 64

6. 121

7. 25

8. 144

_____

Simplify each expression.

9. $\sqrt{32+17}$

10. $\sqrt{100-19}$

11. $\sqrt{64+36}$

12. $\sqrt{73-48}$

_____

13. $2\sqrt{64}+10$

14. $36-\sqrt{36}$

15. $\sqrt{100}-\sqrt{25}$

16. $\sqrt{121}+16$

_____

17. $\sqrt{\dfrac{25}{4}}+\dfrac{1}{2}$

18. $\sqrt{\dfrac{100}{25}}$

19. $\sqrt{\dfrac{196}{49}}$

20. $3(\sqrt{144}-6)$

_____

The Pyramids of Egypt are often called the first wonder of the world. This group of pyramids consists of Menkaura, Khufu, and Khafra. The largest of these is Khufu, sometimes called Cheops. During this time in history, each monarch had his own pyramid built to bury his mummified body. Cheops was a king of Egypt in the early 26th century B.C. His pyramid's original height is estimated to have been 482 ft. It is now approximately 450 ft. The estimated completion date of this structure was 2660 B.C.

21. If the area of the base of Cheops' pyramid is 570,025 ft^2, what is the length of one of the sides of the ancient structure?

    (Hint: $s = \sqrt{A}$)

    _____

22. If a replica of the pyramid were built with a base area of 625 in^2, what would be the length of each side?

    (Hint: $s = \sqrt{A}$)

    _____

Exponents and Roots

LESSON 6

Practice B: Estimating Square Roots

Each square root is between two consecutive integers. Name the integers. Explain your answer.

1. $\sqrt{6}$

_____

2. $\sqrt{20}$

_____

3. $\sqrt{28}$

_____

4. $\sqrt{44}$

_____

5. $\sqrt{31}$

_____

6. $\sqrt{52}$

_____

7. The area of a square piece of cardboard is 70 cm². What is the approximate length of each side of the cardboard?

_____

Approximate each square root to the nearest hundredth.

8. $\sqrt{63}$

9. $\sqrt{18}$

10. $\sqrt{87}$

11. $\sqrt{319}$

Use a calculator to find each value. Round to the nearest tenth.

12. $\sqrt{14}$

13. $\sqrt{42}$

14. $\sqrt{21}$

15. $\sqrt{47}$

16. $\sqrt{58}$

17. $\sqrt{60}$

18. $\sqrt{35}$

19. $\sqrt{75}$

Holt McDougal Mathematics

LESSON 7 — Exponents and Roots

Practice B: The Real Numbers

Write all names that apply to each number.

1. $-\dfrac{7}{8}$

2. $\sqrt{0.15}$

3. $\sqrt{\dfrac{18}{2}}$

_____

_____

4. $\sqrt{45}$

5. -25

6. -6.75

_____

_____

State if the number is rational, irrational, or not a real number.

7. $\sqrt{14}$

8. $\sqrt{-16}$

9. $\dfrac{6.2}{0}$

10. $\sqrt{49}$

_____

11. $\dfrac{7}{20}$

12. $-\sqrt{81}$

13. $\sqrt{\dfrac{7}{9}}$

14. -1.3

_____

Find a real number between each pair of numbers.

15. $7\dfrac{3}{5}$ and $7\dfrac{4}{5}$

16. 6.45 and $\dfrac{13}{2}$

17. $\dfrac{7}{8}$ and $\dfrac{9}{10}$

_____

18. Give an example of a rational number between $-\sqrt{4}$ and $\sqrt{4}$

_____

19. Give an example of an irrational number less than 0.

_____

20. Give an example of a number that is not real.

_____

Holt McDougal Mathematics

LESSON 8

Exponents and Roots
Practice B: The Pythagorean Theorem

Find the length of the hypotenuse to the nearest tenth.

1.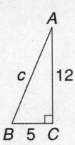

_____

2.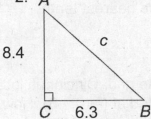

_____

3.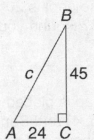

_____

Solve for the unknown side in each right triangle to the nearest tenth.

4.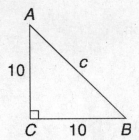

_____

5.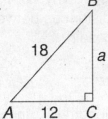

_____

6.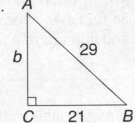

_____

7.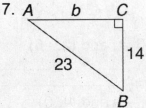

_____

8.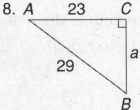

_____

9.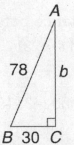

_____

10. A glider flies 8 miles south from the airport and then 15 miles east. Then it flies in a straight line back to the airport. What was the distance of the glider's last leg back to the airport?

_____

Holt McDougal Mathematics

LESSON 9 **Exponents and Roots**
Practice B: Applying the Pythagorean Theorem and its Converse

1. The length of a rectangular swimming pool is 50 feet. The width of the pool is 20 feet. What is the length of the diagonal of the pool? Round your answer to the nearest tenth.

   _____

2. A map is placed on a coordinate grid. Cincinnati located at (5, 4) and San Diego is located at (−10, −3). How far apart is Cincinnati from San Diego on the map? Round your answer to the nearest tenth.

   _____

3. Katie, Ralph, and Juan are tossing a football. Katie is 22.5 feet away from Ralph. Ralph is 58.5 feet away from Juan. Juan is 54 feet away from Katie. Do the distances between Katie, Ralph, and Juan form a right triangle? Explain.

   _____

4. A rectangular picture from has a length of 7 inches and a width of 5 inches. What is the length of the diagonal of the picture frame? Round your answer to the nearest tenth.

   _____

Find the distance between the two points to the nearest tenth.

5. (0, 5) and (−4, 2)   6. (1, 9) and (6, 3)   7. (−6, 4) and (2, −6)

_____   _____   _____

8. (−1, −7) and (−3, −5)   9. (4, 0) and (−9, 7)   10. (0, −8) and (4, 0)

_____   _____   _____

Tell whether the given side lengths form a right triangle.

11. 7, 24, 25   12. 30, 40, 45   13. 21.6, 28.8, 36

_____   _____   _____

14. 10, 15, 18   15. 10.5, 36, 50   16. 2.5, 6, 6.5

_____   _____   _____

LESSON 1

Ratios, Proportions, and Similarity

Practice B: Ratios, Rates, and Unit Rates

1. Copper weighing 4480 kilograms has a volume of 0.5 cubic meters. What is the density of copper?

   _____

2. Yoshi's yogurt contains 15 calories per ounce. How many calories are in an 8-ounce container of Yoshi's yogurt?

   _____

3. Emily earns $7.50 per hour. How much does she earn in 3 hours?

   _____

4. An antelope can run 152.5 miles in 2.5 hours. What is average speed of the antelope?

   _____

5. Bob and Marquis went on a trip. The first day, they drove 465 miles in 8 hours. What is their average speed for the first day of their trip?

   _____

6. A racecar was attempting to set a record. The racecar went 1000 feet in 4.5 seconds. To the nearest tenth, what is the average speed of the racecar?

   _____

Tell which is the better buy.

7. 8.2 oz of toothpaste for $2.99 or 6.4 oz of toothpaste for $2.49

   _____

8. a 3 lb bag of apples for $2.99 or a 5 lb bag of apples for $4.99

   _____

9. 16 oz bottle of soda for $1.25 or 20 oz bottle of soda for $1.55

   _____

10. Mavis rides the bus every day. She bought a bus pass good for the month of October for $38.75. How much was Mavis charged per day for the bus pass?

    _____

Holt McDougal Mathematics

Ratios, Proportions, and Similarity

LESSON 2

Practice B: Solving Proportions

Tell whether the ratios are proportional.

1. $\dfrac{3}{4} \overset{?}{=} \dfrac{9}{12}$

2. $\dfrac{9}{24} \overset{?}{=} \dfrac{18}{48}$

3. $\dfrac{16}{24} \overset{?}{=} \dfrac{10}{18}$

4. $\dfrac{13}{25} \overset{?}{=} \dfrac{26}{50}$

5. $\dfrac{10}{32} \overset{?}{=} \dfrac{16}{38}$

6. $\dfrac{20}{36} \overset{?}{=} \dfrac{50}{90}$

7. $\dfrac{20}{28} \overset{?}{=} \dfrac{28}{36}$

8. $\dfrac{14}{42} \overset{?}{=} \dfrac{16}{36}$

9. A karate team had 6 girls and 9 boys. Then 2 more girls and 3 more boys joined the team. Did the ratio of girls to boys stay the same? Explain.

_____

10. Janessa bought 4 stamps for $1.48. At this rate, how much would 10 stamps cost?

_____

11. Janelle can mow 5 lawns in 36 minutes. At this rate, how long will it take her to mow 11 lawns?

_____

12. An animal shelter wants their ratio of dogs to cats to be 3:2. If the animal shelter has 78 dogs, how many cats should they have?

_____

13. On a field trip, the ratio of teachers to students must be 2:9. If there are 81 students on the field trip, how many teachers must there be?

_____

14. A gallery owner is hanging up 444 pictures for an art exhibit. She has put up 37 pictures in 9 minutes. If she continues at the same rate how many more minutes will it take her to hang the rest of the pictures?

_____

LESSON
3

Ratios, Proportions, and Similarity

Practice B: Similar Figures

1. Which triangles are similar?

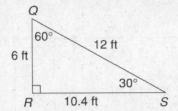 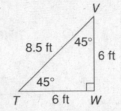 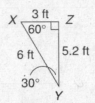

_____

2. A photo is 12 in. wide by 18 in. tall. If the width is scaled down to 9 inches, how tall should the similar photo be?

_____

3. An isosceles triangle has a base of 20 cm and legs measuring 36 cm. How long are the legs of a similar triangle with base measuring 50 cm?

_____

4. A picture of a school's mascot is 18 in. wide and 24 in. long. It is enlarged proportionally to banner size. If the width is enlarged to 63 in., what is the length of the banner?

_____

5. Carol has a 24 cm × 36 cm photo that she reduces to $\frac{3}{4}$ of its size. What are the dimensions of the new photo?

_____

6. Erik is drawing a picture of his school's basketball court. The actual basketball court is 84 ft long and 50 ft wide. If Erik draws the court with a length of 21 in., what will be the width?

_____

7. The Henry Ford Museum in Dearborn, Michigan hosts a theater with one of the world's largest screens, which is 60 ft × 84 ft. If a classroom projection screen were changed to be in direct proportion with the screen at the Henry Ford Museum, the dimensions would be 5 ft × _____ ft.

_____

LESSON	Ratios, Proportions, and Similarity
4	Practice B: Dilations

Tell whether each transformation is a dilation.

1.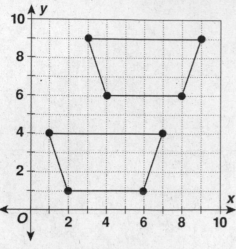

_____

2.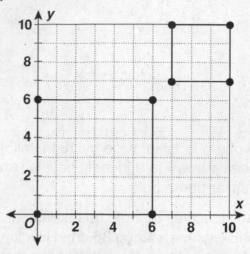

_____

Dilate each figure by the given scale factor with the origin as the center of dilation. What are the vertices of the image?

3. scale factor of 2

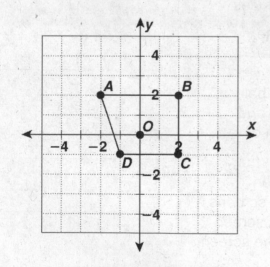

_____

4. scale factor of $\frac{1}{2}$

10

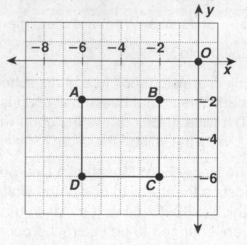

_____

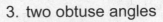

LESSON
1
Geometric Relationships
Practice B: Angle Relationships

Use the diagram to name each figure.

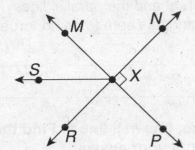

1. a right angle

   _____

2. two acute angles

   _____

3. two obtuse angles

   _____

4. a pair of complementary angles

   _____

   _____

   _____

5. three pairs of supplementary angles

   _____

   _____

   _____

Use the diagram to find each angle measure.

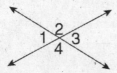

6. If m∠2 = 110°, find m∠4.

   _____   7. If m∠1 = n°, find m∠3.

   _____

8. The diagram shows the intersection of three
   roadways on a map. Based on the diagram, what
   should be the measure of ∠ECD?

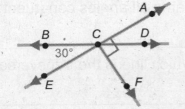

LESSON
2

Geometric Relationships
Practice B: Parallel and Perpendicular Lines

1. Measure the angles formed by the transversal and the parallel lines. Which angles seem to be congruent?

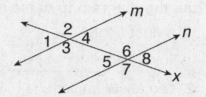

_____

_____

In the figure, line *m* || line *n*. Find the measure of each angle. Justify your answer.

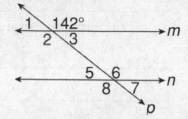

2. ∠1

3. ∠2

_____   _____

4. ∠5

5. ∠6

_____   _____

6. ∠8

7. ∠7

_____   _____

In the figure, line *a* || line *b*. Find the measure of each angle. Justify your answer.

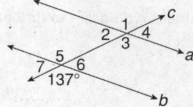

8. ∠2

9. ∠5

_____   _____

10. ∠6

11. ∠7

_____   _____

12. ∠4

13. ∠3

_____   _____

In the figure, line *r* || line *s*.

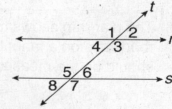

14. Name all angles congruent to ∠2.

_____

15. Which line is the transversal?

_____

Holt McDougal Mathematics

LESSON 3

Geometric Relationships

Practice B: Triangles

1. Find $x°$ in the right triangle.

_____

2. Find $y°$ in the obtuse triangle.

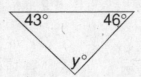

_____

3. Find $m°$ in the acute triangle.

_____

4. Find $w°$ in the acute triangle.

_____

5. Find $t°$ in the scalene triangle.

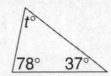

_____

6. Find $n°$ in the scalene triangle.

_____

7. Find $x°$ in the isosceles triangle.

_____

8. Find y in the equilateral triangle.

_____

9. Find r in the isosceles triangle.

_____

10. The second angle in a triangle is one third as large as the first. The third angle is two thirds as large as the first angle. Find the angle measures. Draw a possible picture of the triangle.

_____

Tell whether a triangle can have sides with the given lengths. Explain.

11. 6 ft, 8 ft, 13 ft   12. 15 cm, 8 cm, 2 cm   13. 9 mm, 22 mm, 14 mm

_____   _____   _____

Holt McDougal Mathematics

LESSON 4	**Geometric Relationships**
	Practice B: Coordinate Geometry

Graph the polygons with the given vertices. Give the most specific name for each polygon.

1. $S(-3, -3)$, $T(-3, 4)$, $U(4, -3)$

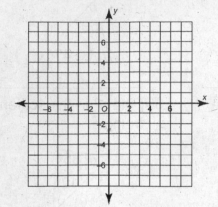

_____

2. $M(-1, 2)$, $N(2, 0)$, $Q(2, -4)$, $P(-1, -2)$

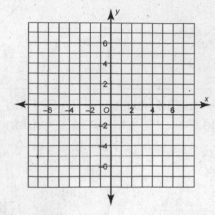

_____

Find the coordinates of each missing vertex.

3. Triangle WUV has a right angle at W and $WU = 5$.

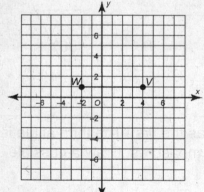

_____

4. Quadrilateral $JKLM$ is a square.

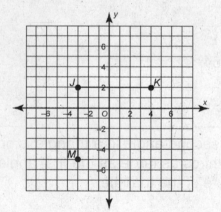

_____

Find the coordinates of the midpoint of each segment.

5. $\overline{XY}$ with endpoints $X(1, 2)$ and $Y(4, 5)$ _____

6. $\overline{ST}$ with endpoints $S(-8, 6)$ and $T(2, 4)$ _____

7. $\overline{FG}$ with endpoints $F(3, 9)$ and $G(-5, 6)$ _____

8. $\overline{LP}$ with endpoints $L(6, 0)$ and $P(-3, -4)$ _____

9. $\overline{EC}$ with endpoints $E(-2, -8)$ and $C(-1, -7)$ _____

Holt McDougal Mathematics

Geometric Relationships

LESSON 5

Practice B: Congruence

Write a congruence statement for each pair of congruent polygons.

1.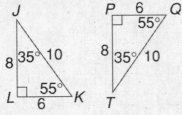

   _____

2.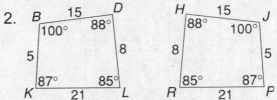

   _____

3.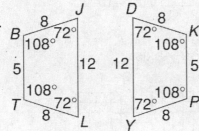

   _____

4.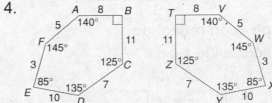

   _____

In the figure, triangle *PRT* ≅ triangle *FJH*.

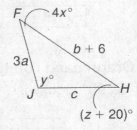

5. Find *a*.

   _____

6. Find *b*.

   _____

7. Find *c*.

   _____

8. Find *x*.

   _____

9. Find *y*.

   _____

10. Find *z*.

   _____

LESSON
6

Geometric Relationships

Practice B: Transformations

Graph each translation.

1. 3 units left and 9 units down

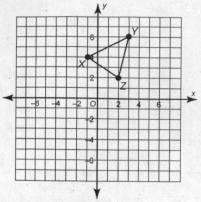

2. 3 units right and 6 units up

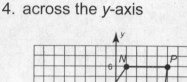

Graph each reflection.

3. across the *x*-axis

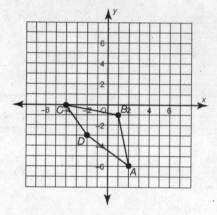

4. across the *y*-axis

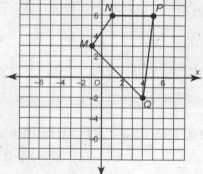

Graph each rotation around the origin.

5. 90° clockwise

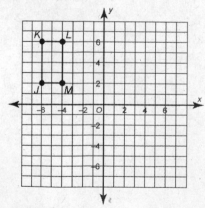

6. 180°

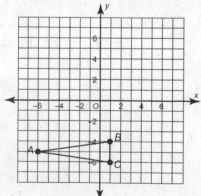

7. A parallelogram has vertices *A*(−1, 3), *B*(4, 3), *C*(6, −1), and *D*(1, −1). After a transformation, the coordinates of the image are *A'* (1, 3), *B'* (−4, 3), *C'* (−6, −1), and *D'* (−1, −1). Describe the transformation. _____

Holt McDougal Mathematics

© Houghton Mifflin Harcourt Publishing Company

LESSON	**Geometric Relationships**
7	**Practice B: Similarity and Congruence Transformations**

Identify each transformation from the original to the image, and tell whether the two figures are similar or congruent.

1. Original: $A(0, 2)$, $B(3, 4)$, $C(7, -2)$, $D(4, -4)$

   Image: $A'(0, -2)$, $B'(-3, -4)$, $C'(-7, 2)$, $D'(-4, 4)$

   _____

2. Original: $A(-3, -4)$, $B(-1, -2)$, $C(1, -4)$, $D(0, -7)$, $E(-2, -7)$

   Image: $A'(2, -5)$, $B'(4, -3)$, $C'(6, -5)$, $D'(5, -8)$, $E'(3, -8)$

   _____

3. Original: $A(-3, -3)$, $B(-2, 3)$, $C(2, -2)$

   Image: $A'(-9, -9)$, $B'(-6, 6)$, $C'(6, -6)$

   _____

4. Original: $A(-4, 8)$, $B(4, 7)$, $C(-4, 6)$

   Image: $A'(-4, -8)$, $B'(4, -7)$, $C'(-4, -6)$

   _____

5. Original: $A(5, -2)$, $B(8, -2)$, $C(8, -7)$, $D(5, -7)$

   Image: $A'(-2, -5)$, $B'(-2, -8)$, $C'(-7, -8)$, $D'(-7, -5)$

   _____

6. Original: $A(-5, -5)$, $B(4, 1)$, $C(4, -6)$

   Image: $A'(5, -5)$, $B'(-4, 1)$, $C'(-4, -6)$

   _____

7. Original: $A(-9, -6)$, $B(6, 3)$, $C(3, -9)$

   Image: $A'(-6, -4)$, $B'(4, 2)$, $C'(2, -6)$

   _____

8. Original: $A(-4, 4)$, $B(0, 6)$, $C(4, -2)$, $D(1, -1)$

   Image: $A'(-4, -4)$, $B'(-6, 0)$, $C'(2, 4)$, $D'(1, 1)$

   _____

  Holt McDougal Mathematics

LESSON 8 Geometric Relationships

Practice B: Identifying Combined Transformations

Identify the combined transformations from the original to the final image, and tell whether the two figures are similar or congruent.

1.

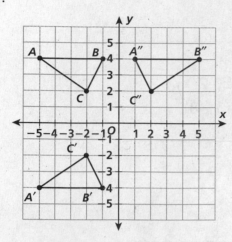

_____

2.

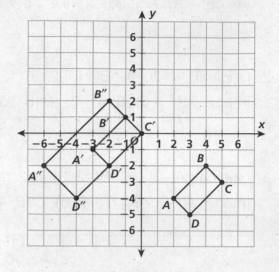

_____

Find a sequence of at least two combined transformations for transforming the original to the final image. Justify your answer.

3.

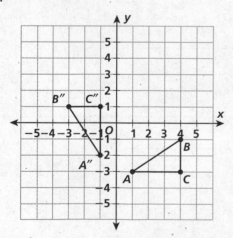

_____

4.

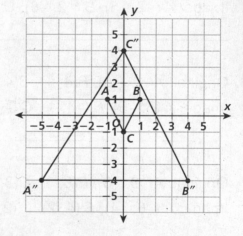

_____

LESSON
1

Measurement and Geometry

Practice B: Circles

Find the circumference of each circle, both in terms of π and to the nearest tenth. Use 3.14 for π.

1. circle with radius 10 in.

_____

2. circle with diameter 13 cm

_____

3. circle with diameter 18 m

_____

4. circle with radius 15 ft

_____

5. circle with radius 11.5 in.

_____

6. circle with diameter 16.4 cm

_____

Find the area of each circle, both in terms of π and to the nearest tenth. Use 3.14 for π.

7. circle with radius 9 in.

_____

8. circle with diameter 14 cm

_____

9. circle with radius 20 ft

_____

10. circle with diameter 17 m

_____

11. circle with diameter 15.4 m

_____

12. circle with radius 22 yd

_____

13. Graph a circle with center (0, 0) that passes through (0, –3). Find the area and circumference, both in terms of π and to the nearest tenth. Use 3.14 for π.

_____

_____

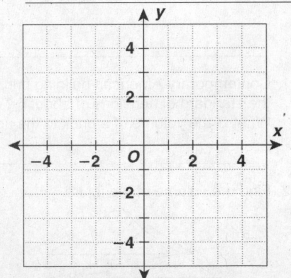

14. A wheel has a radius of $2\frac{1}{3}$ feet. About how far does it travel if it makes 60 complete revolutions? Use $\frac{22}{7}$ for π.

_____

© Houghton Mifflin Harcourt Publishing Company

Holt McDougal Mathematics

Measurement and Geometry

Practice B: Volume of Prisms and Cylinders

Find the volume of each figure to the nearest tenth. Use 3.14 π.

1.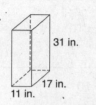
22 in. 42 in. 22 in.

_____

2. 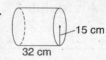 6.5 cm
16 cm

_____

3.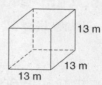
13 m
13 m
13 m

_____

4.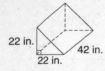
6 cm
45 cm 12 cm

_____

5.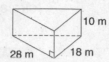
10 m
28 m 18 m

_____

6.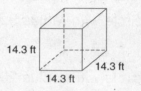
15 cm
32 cm

_____

7.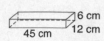
31 in.
17 in.
11 in.

_____

8.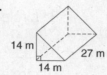
14 m
27 m
14 m

_____

9.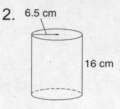
14.3 ft
14.3 ft
14.3 ft

_____

10. A cylinder has a radius of 6 ft and a height of 25 ft. Explain whether tripling the height will triple the volume of the cylinder.

_____

_____

11. Contemporary American building bricks are rectangular blocks with the standard dimensions of about 5.7 cm by 9.5 cm by 20.3 cm. What is the volume of a brick to the nearest tenth of a unit?

_____

12. Find the volume of the figure.

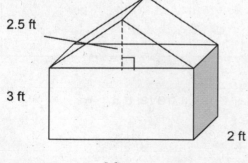
2.5 ft
3 ft
2 ft
6 ft

_____

LESSON 3 Measurement and Geometry

Practice B: Volume of Pyramids and Cones

Find the volume of each figure to the nearest tenth. Use 3.14 for π.

1.
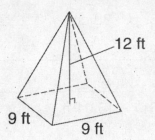
12 ft
9 ft   9 ft

_____

2.
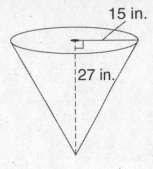
15 in.
27 in.

_____

3.
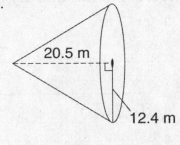
20.5 m
12.4 m

_____

4.
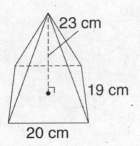
23 cm
19 cm
20 cm

_____

5.
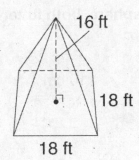
16 ft
18 ft
18 ft

_____

6.
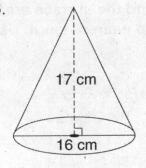
17 cm
16 cm

_____

7. The base of a regular pyramid has an area of 28 in^2. The height of the pyramid is 15 in. Find the volume.

_____

8. The radius of a cone is 19.4 cm and its height is 24 cm. Find the volume of the cone to the nearest tenth.

_____

9. Find the volume of a rectangular pyramid if the height is 13 m and the base sides are 12 m and 15 m.

_____

10. A funnel has a diameter of 9 in. and is 16 in. deep. Use a calculator to find the volume of the funnel to the nearest hundredth.

_____

11. A square pyramid has a height 18 cm and a base that measures 12 cm on each side. Explain whether tripling the height would triple the volume of the pyramid.

_____

_____

_____

Holt McDougal Mathematics

LESSON 4 · Measurement and Geometry

Practice B: Spheres

Find the volume of each sphere, both in terms of π and to the nearest tenth. Use 3.14 for π.

1. $r = 9$ ft

_____

_____

2. $r = 21$ m

_____

_____

3. $d = 30$ cm

_____

_____

4. $d = 24$ cm

_____

_____

5. $r = 15.4$ in.

_____

_____

6. $r = 16.01$ ft

_____

_____

Find the surface area of each sphere, both in terms of π and to the nearest tenth. Use 3.14 for π.

7.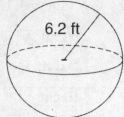
6.2 ft

_____

_____

8.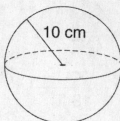
10 cm

_____

_____

9.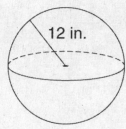
12 in.

_____

_____

10.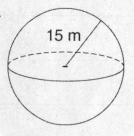
15 m

_____

_____

11.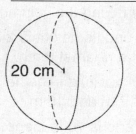
20 cm

_____

_____

12.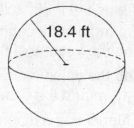
18.4 ft

_____

_____

13. Compare the volume and surface area of a sphere with diameter 3 m with that of a cylinder with height 1.5 m and a base with radius 1 ft.

_____

_____

Holt McDougal Mathematics

LESSON 1 Multi-Step Equations
Practice B: Simplifying Algebraic Expressions

Combine like terms.

1. $8a^3 - 5a^3$

2. $12g + 7g$

3. $4a + 7a + 6$

4. $6x + 3y + 5x$

5. $10k - 3k + 5h$

6. $3p^6 - 7q + 14p^6$

7. $3k + 7k + 5k^2$

8. $5c + 12d - 6$

9. $13 + 4b + 6b - 5$

10. $4f + 6 + 7f - 2$

11. $x^3 + y + 3x^3 + 7y$

12. $9n + 13 - 8n - 6$

Simplify.

13. $4(x + 3) - 5$

14. $6(7 + x) + 5x$

15. $3(5 + 3x) - 4x$

Solve.

16. $6y + 2y = 16$

17. $14b - 9b = 35$

18. $3q + 9q = 48$

19. Gregg has q quarters and p pennies. His brother has 4 times as many quarters and 8 times as many pennies as Gregg has. Write the sum of the number of coins they have, and then combine like terms.

_____

20. If Gregg has 6 quarters and 15 pennies, how many total coins do Gregg and his brother have?

_____

Holt McDougal Mathematics

LESSON
2

Multi-Step Equations
Practice B: Solving Multi-Step Equations

Solve.

1. $2x + 5x + 4 = 25$

2. $9 + 3y - 2y = 14$

3. $16 = 2(2w + w - 1)$

_____

4. $26 = 3b - 2 - 7b$

5. $31 + 4t - t = 40$

6. $2(7 - x) + 4x = 20$

_____

7. $\dfrac{5m}{8} - \dfrac{6}{8} + \dfrac{3m}{8} = \dfrac{2}{8}$

8. $-4\dfrac{2}{3} = \dfrac{2n}{3} + \dfrac{1}{3} + \dfrac{n}{3}$

9. $7a + 16 - 3a = -4$

_____

10. $\dfrac{x}{2} + 1 + \dfrac{3x}{4} = -9$

11. $7m + 3 - 4m = -9$

12. $\dfrac{2x}{5} + 3 - \dfrac{4x}{5} = \dfrac{1}{5}$

_____

13. $\dfrac{7k}{8} - \dfrac{3}{4} - \dfrac{5k}{16} = \dfrac{3}{8}$

14. $3(2y + 3) - 4y = -3$

15. $\dfrac{5a}{6} - \dfrac{7}{12} + \dfrac{3a}{4} = -2\dfrac{1}{6}$

_____

16. The measure of an angle is 28° greater than its complement.
Find the measure of each angle.

_____

17. The measure of an angle is 21° more than twice its supplement.
Find the measure of each angle.

_____

18. The perimeter of the triangle is 126 units.
Find the measure of each side.

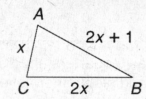

_____

_____

19. The base angles of an isosceles triangle
are congruent. If the measure of each of
the base angles is twice the measure of
the third angle, find the measure of all
three angles.

_____

LESSON
3

Multi-Step Equations

Practice B: Solving Equations with Variables on Both Sides

Solve.

1. $7x - 11 = -19 + 3x$

2. $11a + 9 = 4a + 30$

3. $4t + 14 = \dfrac{6t}{5} + 7$

_____

_____

_____

4. $\dfrac{3y}{8} - 9 = 13 + \dfrac{y}{8}$

5. $\dfrac{3k}{5} + 44 = \dfrac{12k}{25} + 8$

6. $15 - x = 2(x + 3)$

_____

_____

_____

7. $15y + 14 = 2(5y + 6)$

8. $14 - \dfrac{w}{8} = \dfrac{3w}{4} - 21$

9. $\dfrac{1}{2}(6x - 4) = 4x - 9$

_____

_____

_____

10. $4(3d - 2) = 8d - 5$

11. $\dfrac{y}{3} + 11 = \dfrac{y}{2} - 3$

12. $\dfrac{2x - 9}{3} = 8 - 3x$

_____

_____

_____

13. Forty-eight decreased by a number is the same as the difference of four times the number and seven. Find the number.

_____

14. The square and the equilateral triangle at the right have the same perimeter. Find the length of the sides of the triangle.

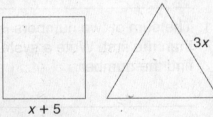

$3x$

$x + 5$

_____

15. The equation $V = \dfrac{1}{3} Bh$ gives the volume V of a pyramid, where B is the area of the base and h is the height. Solve this equation for B.

_____

Holt McDougal Mathematics

Multi-Step Equations

LESSON 4

Practice B: Systems of Equations

Solve each system of equations.

1. $y = 2x - 4$
   $y = x - 1$

   _____

2. $y = -x + 10$
   $y = x + 2$

   _____

3. $y = 2x - 1$
   $y = -3x - 6$

   _____

4. $y = 2x$
   $y = 12 - x$

   _____

5. $y = 2x - 3$
   $y = 2x + 1$

   _____

6. $y = 3x - 1$
   $y = x + 1$

   _____

7. $x + y = 0$
   $5x + 2y = -3$

   _____

8. $2x - 3y = 0$
   $2x + y = 8$

   _____

9. $2x + 3y = 6$
   $4x + 6y = 12$

   _____

10. $6x - y = -14$
    $2x - 3y = 6$

    _____

11. The sum of two numbers is 24. The second number is 6 less than the first. Write a system of equations and solve it to find the number.

    _____

    _____

12. Kerry and Luke biked a total of 18 miles in one weekend. Kerry biked 4 miles more than Luke. Write a system of equations and solve it to find how far each boy biked.

    _____

    _____

Holt McDougal Mathematics

**LESSON
1**

Graphing Lines
Practice B: Graphing Linear Equations

Graph each equation and tell whether it is linear.

1. $y = -2x - 5$

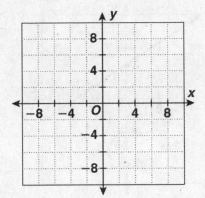

_____

2. $y = -x^2 + 1$

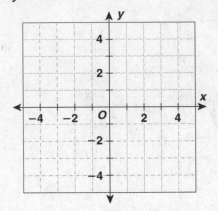

_____

Determine whether the rates of change are constant or variable.

3.

x	0	1	2	4	5
y	3	4	5	6	7

_____

4.

x	2	4	6	8	12
y	7	9	11	13	17

_____

5. A real estate agent commission may be based on the equation $C = 0.06s + 450$, where s represents the total sales. If the agent sells a property for $125,000, what is the commission earned by the agent? Graph the equation and tell whether it is linear.

_____

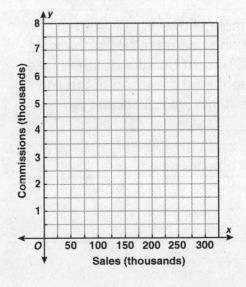

LESSON
2

Graphing Lines

Practice B: Slope of a Line

Find the slope of each line.

1.

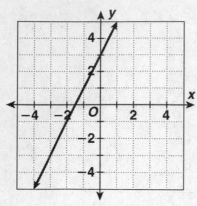

2.

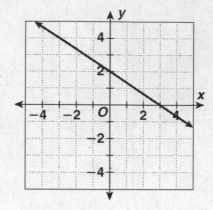

_____   _____

Find the slope of the line that passes through each pair of points.

3. (−2, −8), (1, 4)   4. (−2, 0), (0, 4),   5. (0, 4), (4, 4)   6. (3, −6), (2, −4)

_____   _____   _____   _____

7. (−3, 4), (3, −4)   8. (3, 0), (0, −6),   9. (3, 2), (3, −2)   10. (−4, 4), (3, −1)

_____   _____   _____   _____

11. The table shows the distance
Ms. Long had traveled as she went
to the beach. Use the data to make
a graph. Find the slope of the line
and explain what it shows.

Time (min)	Distance (mi)
8	6
12	9
16	12
20	15

_____

_____

_____

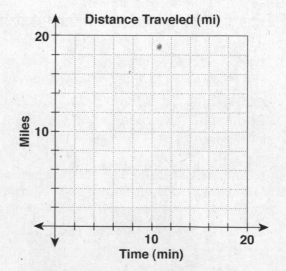

© Houghton Mifflin Harcourt Publishing Company

LESSON
3

Graphing Lines

Practice B: Using Slopes and Intercepts

**Find the *x*-intercept and *y*-intercept of each line.
Use the intercepts to graph the equation.**

1. $x - y = -3$

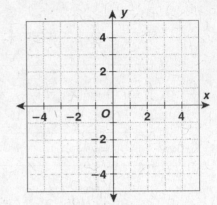

2. $2x + 3y = 12$

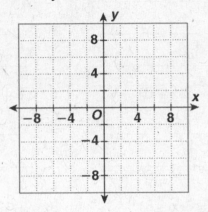

_____

_____

**Write each equation in slope-intercept form, and then find the
slope and *y*-intercept.**

3. $3x + y = 0$ 4. $2x - y = -15$ 5. $x - 5y = 10$

_____   _____   _____

_____   _____   _____

**Write the equation of the line that passes through each pair of
points in slope-intercept form.**

6. $(3, 4), (4, 6)$ 7. $(-1, -1), (2, -10)$ 8. $(6, 5), (-9, -20)$

_____   _____   _____

9. A pizzeria charges $8 for a large
cheese pizza, plus $2 for each topping.
The total cost for a large pizza is given
by the equation $C = 2t + 8$, where t is
the number of toppings. Graph the
equation for t between 0 and 5 toppings,
and explain the meaning of the slope
and *y*-intercept.

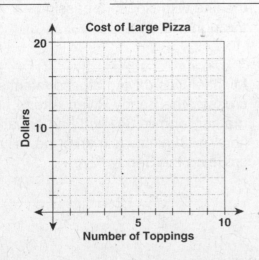

_____

_____

LESSON
4

Graphing Lines
Practice B: Point-Slope Form

Use the point-slope form of each equation to identify a point the line passes through and the slope of the line.

1. $y - 2 = 4(x - 1)$

_____

_____

2. $y + 1 = 2(x - 3)$

_____

_____

3. $y - 4 = -3(x + 1)$

_____

_____

4. $y + 5 = -2(x + 6)$

_____

_____

5. $y + 4 = -9(x + 3)$

_____

_____

6. $y - 7 = -7(x - 7)$

_____

_____

7. $y - 10 = 6(x - 8)$

_____

_____

8. $y + 12 = 2.5(x + 4)$

_____

_____

9. $y + 8 = \dfrac{1}{2}(x - 3)$

_____

_____

Write the point-slope form of the equation with the given slope that passes through the indicated point.

10. the line with slope −1 passing through (2, 5)

_____

11. the line with slope 2 passing through (−1, 4)

_____

12. the line with slope 4 passing through (−3, −2)

_____

13. the line with slope 3 passing through (7, −6)

_____

14. the line with slope −3 passing through (−6, 4)

_____

15. the line with slope −2 passing through (5, 1)

_____

16. Michael was driving at a constant speed of 60 mph when he crossed the Sandy River. After 1 hour, he passed a highway marker for mile 84. Write an equation in point-slope form, and find which highway marker he will pass 90 minutes after crossing the Sandy River.

_____

Graphing Lines

Practice B: Direct Variation

Determine whether the data sets show direct variation.

1.

x	y
6	9
4	6
0	0
−2	−3
−8	−12

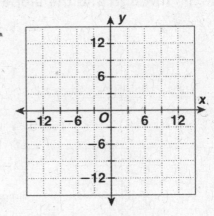

_____

2. Write the equation of direct variation for Exercise 1.

_____

Find each equation of direct variation, given that y varies with x.

3. y is 32 when x is 4

_____

4. y is −10 when x is −20

_____

5. y is 63 when x is −7

_____

6. y is 40 when x is 50

_____

7. y is 87.5 when x is 25

_____

8. y is 90 when x is 270

_____

9. The table shows the length and width of various U.S. flags. Determine whether there is direct variation between the two data sets. If so, find the equation of direct variation.

Length (ft)	2.85	5.7	7.6	9.88	11.4
Width (ft)	1.5	3	4	5.2	6

_____

_____

_____

Holt McDougal Mathematics

LESSON
6

Graphing Lines

Practice B: Solving Systems of Linear Equations by Graphing

Solve each linear system by graphing. Check your answer.

1. $y = -1$
   $y = 2x - 7$

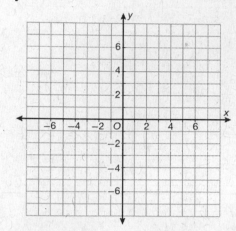

2. $x - y = 6$
   $2x = 12 + 2y$

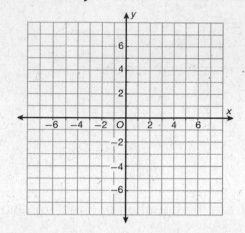

3. $\frac{1}{2}x - y = 4$
   $2y = x + 6$

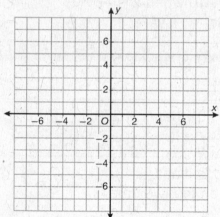

4. $y = 4x - 3$
   $2y - 3x = -4$

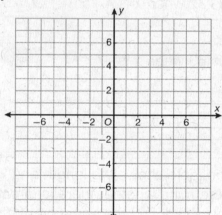

5. Two skaters are racing toward the finish line of a race. The first skater has a 40 meter lead and is traveling at a rate of 12 meters per second. The second skater is traveling at a rate of 14 meters per second. How long will it take for the second skater to pass the first skater?

_____

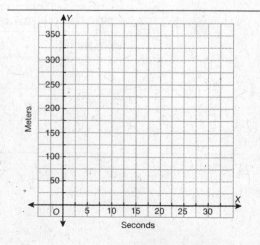

Holt McDougal Mathematics

Data, Prediction, and Linear Functions

LESSON 1

Practice B: Scatter Plots

1. Use the given data to make a scatter plot, and describe the correlation.

Tall Buildings in U.S. Cities

Building	City	Stories	Height (meters)
Sears Tower	Chicago	110	442
Empire State Building	New York	102	381
Bank of America Plaza	Atlanta	55	312
Library Tower	Los Angeles	75	310
Key Tower	Cleveland	57	290
Columbia Seafirst Center	Seattle	76	287
NationsBank Plaza	Dallas	72	281
NationsBank Corporate Center	Charlotte	60	265

Tall Buildings in U.S. Cities

2. Make a scatter plot of the data, and draw a line of best fit. Then use the data to predict the percentage of American homeowners in 1955.

Percent of Americans Owning Homes

Year	1950	1960	1970	1980	1990
Percent	55.0%	61.9%	62.9%	64.4%	64.2%

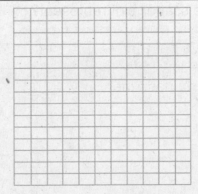

Holt McDougal Mathematics

LESSON 2 Data, Prediction, and Linear Functions

Practice B: Linear Best Fit Models

Use the scatter plot for Exercises 1–6.

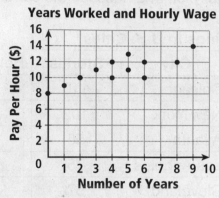

Years Worked and Hourly Wage

1. Does the pattern of association between year and pay per hour appear to be linear or nonlinear?

   _____

2. Identify any clustering.

   _____

3. Identify any possible outliers.

   _____

4. Write an equation for the line of best fit.

   _____

5. What does the slope in the scatter plot represent?

   _____

   _____

6. What does the *y*-intercept in the scatter plot represent?

   _____

   _____

LESSON 3

Data, Prediction, and Linear Functions

Practice B: Linear Functions

Determine whether each function is linear. If so, give the slope and y-intercept of the function's graph.

1. $f(x) = -3x + 2$

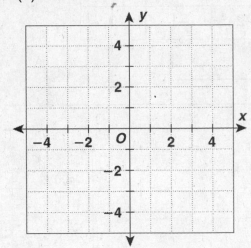

_____

2. $f(x) = x^2 - 1$

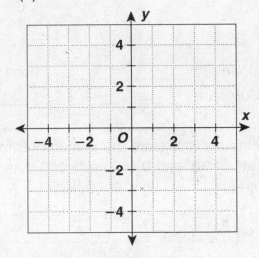

_____

Write a rule for each linear function.

3.

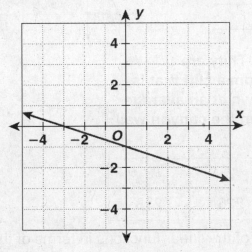

_____

4.

x	y
-3	16
-1	12
3	4
7	-4

_____

5. At the Sweater Store, the price of a sweater is 20% more than the wholesale cost, plus a markup of $8. Find a rule for a linear function that describes the price of sweaters at the Sweater Store. Use it to determine the price of a sweater with a wholesale cost of $24.50.

_____

_____

Name _____ Date _____ Class_____

Data, Prediction, and Linear Functions
Practice B: Comparing Multiple Representations

1. Find and compare the slopes for the linear functions *f* and *g*.

$f(x) = \dfrac{1}{2}x - 4$

x	−4	0	4	8
g(x)	−3	−2	−1	0

slope of *f* _____ slope of *g* _____

Compare _____

_____

2. Find and compare the *y*-intercepts for the linear functions *f* and *g*.

x	−1	0	1	2
f(x)	−7	−2	3	8

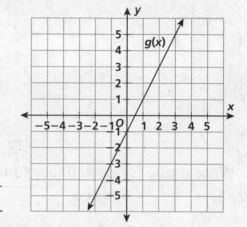

y-intercept of *f* _____

y-intercept of *g* _____

Compare _____

_____

Connor and Sheila are in a rock-climbing club. They are climbing down a canyon wall. Connor starts from a cliff that is 200 feet above the canyon floor and climbs down at an average speed of 10 feet per minute. Sheila climbs down the canyon wall as shown in the table.

Time (min)	0	1	2	3
Sheila's height (ft)	242	234	226	218

3. Interpret the rates of change and initial values of the linear functions in terms of the situations they model.

<u>Connor</u>

Initial value _____

Rate of change _____

Compare _____

_____

<u>Sheila</u>

Initial value _____

Rate of change _____